Family Tree designed and illustrated by my son; Kenneth Anthony Hordge II

T0365412

GENERATIONS

KENNETH A. HORDGE SR.

authorHOUSE®

AuthorHouse™ LLC
1663 Liberty Drive
Bloomington, IN 47403
www.authorhouse.com
Phone: 1-800-839-8640

© 2013 Kenneth A. Hordge Sr. All rights reserved.

No part of this book may be reproduced, stored in a retrieval system, or transmitted by any means without the written permission of the author.

Published by AuthorHouse   09/14/2013

ISBN: 978-1-4817-1716-8 (sc)
ISBN: 978-1-4817-1715-1 (e)

Library of Congress Control Number: 2013902694

Any people depicted in stock imagery provided by Thinkstock are models, and such images are being used for illustrative purposes only.
Certain stock imagery © Thinkstock.

This book is printed on acid-free paper.

Because of the dynamic nature of the Internet, any web addresses or links contained in this book may have changed since publication and may no longer be valid. The views expressed in this work are solely those of the author and do not necessarily reflect the views of the publisher, and the publisher hereby disclaims any responsibility for them.

CONTENTS

DEDICATION

I dedicate this book to my Ancestors with a
simple but deep and meaningful expression;
Thank You

MY FAMILY HISTORY

MY NAME IS KENNETH Anthony Hordge Sr. and this is the history of my ancestry. I really don't remember when I started to have a curiosity about my ancestors, I just know that whenever it was it ignited a burning fire of interest that would not cease until I learned all I could about the when, where, and who of how I came to be.

I started where most people start when they are researching their genealogy, questioning my parents about their lives. When I questioned my parents, I learned all kinds of interesting and even shocking facts, along with some mysteries that are still unsolved to this day. The fact that I am an African American means that in some cases what should be simple research turns out to be an extreme challenge. The main challenge is a result of the record keeping, or I should say the lack thereof caused by the Trans Atlantic Slave Trade.

However, I have been extremely fortunate in that my families oral history and the records I was able to find through researching official documents like the census have helped me to uncover my families history back some 190 years. And through the use of modern technology, I have even been able to trace my origins back to the continent of Africa.

The initial reason I started this project was to know more about myself through the knowledge I gained from my genealogical history. Now, I have broadened the idea to include others who may be interested for the same reason and because I sincerely believe that in order to better our chances for a successful future, we have to be willing to learn from the past.

So, I hope you will join me on this journey, and as you learn about my Ancestry, may the spark ignite a fire of curiosity for you about your own. Ultimately it is my hope that we will all see the beginning of a clearer, brighter future because we took the time to learn about the importance of our past.

THIS IS ME

HERE I AM IN Springfield Illinois circa 2007, and at the time 51 years of age. I was born in New York City in the Bronx at around 9:30 pm on May 31, 1956. I spent the first 13 years of my life in New York before my mother moved my sister and me to the Midwestern City of Indianapolis, Indiana. With the exception of the 4 years I served in the military, I lived in Indy for 31 years. While living in Indianapolis I got married and had two sons, Kenneth, and Spencer, and a stepson Thunder. Although Thunder and I are not connected biologically, spiritually he is definitely my son. I now have three grandchildren, Aireana, Kameron, and Kennedy. Aireana is Thunder's daughter, Kameron and Kennedy are Kenneth's children, his son and daughter respectively. Spencer does not yet have any children.

MY FATHER

MY FATHER'S NAME IS Nathaniel Hordge. He was born on December 25th Christmas Day in a little town in the State of Virginia called Glen Wilton. The town is near the source of one of the most famous rivers in the United States, the James River. Glen Wilton is near the border of West Virginia and is surrounded by beautiful green mountains. The area is known for coal mining. I cannot say how my dad's family came to this area. Maybe they were brought there as slaves or it's possible they came on their own after they were free. I am still researching this but I may never know. My dad did not say much else about growing up in Glen Wilton except there was not much to do there.

When he was old enough my father left Glen Wilton and went to Baltimore Maryland to seek employment. He found a job first working at a dry dock and then at a company called Consolidated Laundry. I know he didn't like working at the laundry because as he told me, he would take off every Monday. One time after he'd taken off his supervisor told him that if he took off on a Monday one more time that he would see to it that my father was inducted into the military. My father paid the man no attention and once again took off on a Monday. True to his word the supervisor had my dad drafted into the military. When he was at the military office he told the man in charge that he was from Virginia and could not be sent in through the State of Maryland. However the recruiter informed my dad that it did not matter. The only choice he had was whether he would go to the military from Maryland or if he chose he could go from Virginia, but one way or another he was going. So off he went into the United States Army, doing his basic training in Texas, then being sent to Wichita Falls, and after that to San Antonio. Finally he received orders to go overseas to the Philippines. This was near the end of World War II. Luckily before he was sent into harms way, the United States dropped the Atomic Bomb on Nagasaki, and Hiroshima effectively ending the war. My father told me that while he was in the Philippines he was assigned to guard Japanese prisoners of War. After serving he returned briefly to Virginia but had a bad experience with a group of racist men who happened to be police officers. These men wanted him to ride in a segregated train car but my father refused. He told me that because he refused, they beat him. After that incident my dad decided to leave the south and head to New York City where he thought he might have a better chance at living a decent life. Many African Americans migrated to northern cities from the south for the same reasons as my dad. It was in New York that my mother and father met.

My father was an outgoing individual who knew how to enjoy his life. Dad was known by his friends and family for always being the life of the party. Two of his favorite pastimes were hunting and golf. My mother and father separated before I entered Kindergarten so I did not get to see a lot of him while growing up. Plus, my mother moved with my sisters and me to Indianapolis when I was 13. After that I did not see him again until I turned 20. My dad passed away at the age of 67. Before he left this earth I had the chance to golf and travel with him to Germany and France where we had a great time. Although I did not get to spend a great deal of time with my dad, the times we did spend together were of quality and value that will always be a part of my most cherished memories.

MY MOTHER

My MOTHER WAS BORN in Charleston South Carolina on November 11ᵗʰ Veterans Day. Actually, Veterans Day had not yet become a holiday when my mother was born. Her father and mother named her Vermella, after her grandmother on her father's side of the family. Charleston has a significant place in American History. It is located on the eastern seaboard and was a major port city. It is also where many slaves landed when brought to this land. As a matter of fact, more African slaves entered this country through Charleston than any other port city. This means that it is more than likely my Ancestors on my mother's side of the family came to Charleston directly from Africa.

My mom was always happy to tell me stories about the times when she was a little girl growing up in Charleston. I remember her telling me that she, along with her parents and siblings lived in a house that was right on the banks of the Ashley River. Her father and grandfather would catch fish and crabs for the family to eat. My mom told me that they also had farm animals even though they did not live on a farm. They had chickens, geese, horses and a mule. I still laugh when I remember the story she told me about the mule. She and her sisters would be sitting on their front porch when the mule would come right up to them and show his teeth. This would scare them half to death and they would scream until my grandmother would come out and chase the mule off.

My mother went to school only until the eleventh grade but she was very intelligent. She is the person who is responsible for my curiosity and love of science. Although she never developed it, my mother has a talent for drawing. One day when I was still a boy I was trying to draw a picture of Superman. After becoming frustrated with my inability I approached my mother and asked if she could help me. Mom took a sheet of paper and began drawing my hero. I was amazed at what I saw coming from the hand of my mother. Before this I never knew she had the talent. And that talent has been passed down to my sister Barbara and my son Kenneth. Somehow it skipped right over me.

As an adult my mother had several jobs, one sewing for the Danskin company, cleaning houses and office buildings, working at the First National City Bank in Manhattan although I don't remember what she did there, and working in the test kitchen of the Stokely Van Camp Company in Indianapolis.

My mother has survived the Great Depression, has witnessed the attack on Pearl harbor and the outbreak of World War II, the dropping of the atomic bomb and the ending of World War II, The Korean War, The first television, the Civil rights era, The rise and fall of the Berlin Wall, The Cuban Missile Crisis, Martin Luther Kings I Have a Dream speech and his assassination, the assassination of President John F. Kennedy, the beginning and ending of the Vietnam War, the first human heart transplant, Man landing and walking on the moon, the Women's, Movement, the Aids epidemic, the computer age, the release of Nelson Mandela, the first and second Gulf Wars, the cloning of Dolly the sheep, Pathfinder sending back pictures from Mars, Globalization, The new Millennium, the controversial election of George W. Bush, the September 11 terrorist attacks, Hurricane Katrina, the capture and killing of Saddam Hussein, The election of the first African American President, the Global Economic Crisis, and the capture and killing of Osama bin Laden.

My mom is a 25-year breast cancer survivor, and has within the last six years been diagnosed with bone marrow cancer. Doctors have told my mother that she would not live much longer, especially if she refused to take chemotherapy treatments, which she has refused.

At the time of this writing, my mom is still alive and has just recently celebrated her 93rd birthday.

MY PATERNAL GRANDFATHER

IN THE INTRODUCTION TO this book I mentioned that there were still some unsolved mysteries involving some of my family members. Well my paternal grandfather is one of those mysteries. My father never knew who his father was. He never saw him, or even a picture of him. When he asked his mother about him, she just looked at my father and said: don't you worry about him, I'll take care of you. After that incident, he was never allowed to talk about his father. Although I have discovered a few more details that I'll mention when I write about my grandmother.

MY PATERNAL GRANDMOTHER (HORDGE)

MY PATERNAL GRANDMOTHER'S NAME is Beatrice. I really don't know where she was born but I think it was in Glen Wilton Virginia. I don't know a lot about my father's mother, partly because she was not a very talkative person, and by the time I really thought about sitting down with her and asking about her life, she'd become stricken with Alzheimer's disease and had become too sick to really respond coherently.

But when I interviewed my dad about his life, he told me a story his aunt had relayed to him about his mother. My grandmother had three sisters, Aunt Florence, Aunt Blanche, and Aunt Clara. I was told that my grandmother and her three sisters were eager to leave little Glen Wilton and try to make their lives better somewhere else. The three sisters traveled to the State of Oklahoma, and then to Columbus Ohio before returning to Glen Wilton. When they returned my grandmother was pregnant with my father who wound up being an only child. After being home for a short time they decided to set out once again to try and make a better life for themselves somewhere else. However my dad's grandmother (my great grandmother) Lucy Richards, told my grandmother that my dad was staying with her because the road was no place for a little boy growing up. So my dad was partially raised by his grandmother. To give you an idea of just how small Glen Wilton is, the town has only fifteen black families living there, or so I was told. And there are not many more that are white. I got a chance to visit the town of Glen Wilton when my grandmother died. We buried her behind the church she used to attend, Mt. Beulah Baptist.

My grandma B as we called her was a woman who needed only the simple pleasures of life. She wound up living in New York after my dad moved there. She was a domestic worker whom my brother told me worked for a family with the last name of Alexander. One of the sons of that Family went on to become a prominent military figure, Secretary of the United States Army. After my dad passed away, I visited my grandmother in a nursing home in the Bronx. I did what my father taught me to do for her, I brought her the two simple things that made her happy: ice cream and cookies. My grandma B passed away in 1999 at the age of 97.

My Paternal Great Grandmother (Richards)

My PATERNAL GREAT GRANDMOTHER'S (my grandma B's mother) name was Lucy Richards. Except for the fact that she partially raised my dad when my grandmother went away to attempt to better her life, I don't know much about my great grandmother Lucy. I know that my dad loved and respected her, and that the house he lived in with her burned down on an Easter Sunday morning. I also know that she married a man named Dan Richards who happened to be a deacon in the Baptist church she attended. However, Dan Richards was not my grandmother's father. So like my dad, I am not sure my grandmother knew who her dad was.

MY MATERNAL GRANDFATHER THOMAS

M Y MOTHER'S FATHER'S NAME is David James Thomas, and he too was born in Charleston South Carolina. As you can see, he was a handsome man and ahead of his time when it came to style. He left Charleston with my grandmother and migrated to New York to try his hand at making a better life for his family. After spending some time in the city, he found a house north of the city in Larchmont and Mamaroneck before going back to the city where he settled for good. A story was told to me by one of my cousins that my grandfather did not want to leave his house in Larchmont, but my grandmother insisted because all of her friends lived in the city. Through research I found out that my grandfather spent most of his adult life as an entrepreneur. He had a fleet of taxicabs; a restaurant called Dave's, and was also a handy man. This is where I get my entrepreneurial spirit. In 1980 my family had a big reunion in New York City and my grandfather was the oldest member and therefore the patron of honor. One of the most cherished pictures I have is of my son Kenneth at the age of one month at the reunion in my granddad's arms. At that time they were the youngest and oldest members of our family. Grandfather David's nickname was Sonny. Today my son Kenneth has the same nickname. My Grandfather David died at the age of ninety-five after a long life as a self made man.

MY MATERNAL GREAT GRANDFATHER THOMAS

MY MATERNAL GREAT GRANDFATHER'S, (my grandfather David's father) name was Henry Beauregard. I could not find any information on my great grandfather Henry, just his name and this picture that was left with the family. But through this picture, I can see where his son, my grandfather David got his sense of style. Both men exuded dignity and were ahead of their time when it came to dreaming of a better life for themselves and their families.

My Maternal Great Grandmother Thomas

I KNOW VERY LITTLE about my great grandmother, my grandfather David's mother. In fact the only thing I really know about her is a story my aunt once told me. She had died when my grandfather David was still a young boy. As far as I know, there aren't any pictures of her. However, her name was Vermella, and that is who my mom is named after.

MY MATERNAL GRANDMOTHER
THOMAS/MICHEL

MY GRANDMOTHER'S, NAME IS Josephine Michel. (maiden name, my mother's mother) She was also born in Charleston. She too was pretty stylish and had a pretty smile. I remember her as being a no nonsense kind of woman who's bad side you did not want to find yourself on. I remember visiting my grandmother in the Bronx New York and whenever we were there I would play with my aunt Tilly's dog Master, a big boxer who stayed with my grandmother.

By the time my grandmother passed away, my mother, siblings and I had already moved to Indianapolis. So my mother attended her funeral without my sisters and I because she could not afford to take us all back to New York. My grandmother was only in her 70's when she passed.

MY MATERNAL GREAT GRANDFATHER MICHEL

MY GREAT GRANDFATHER'S NAME was Samuel Michel. (my grandmother Josephine's father) My great grandfather Samuel lived in Charleston South Carolina. All I know about him are the stories my mother told me, that he loved to fish and often times caught fish and crabs for the family to eat. In his spare time he would make and or repair fishing nets. To earn a living, he was what is known as a Cooper, which is a person who makes and sells wooden crab traps. My mother told me that my great grandfather Michel was a mild mannered person who loved his wife, my great grandmother, and affectionately called her by her nickname, Maggie. I do not know what age he was when he passed away but through research I found that he is buried in the Monrovia Cemetery in Charleston South Carolina supposedly next to his wife, my Great grandmother.

My Maternal Great Grandmother Michel/Smalls

MY GREAT GRANDMOTHER'S NAME was Willie Ann. (Josephine's mother) I know, it is an unusual name for a woman and I've always wondered what caused her parents to give her such a name. Perhaps she was named for a prominent male in the family or maybe even a good family friend. I really don't know but the mystery remains to this day. All I really know is that after Willie Ann, the trail runs cold in terms of information about her parents. I certainly don't know their names and my research gives only slight clues as to where they may have lived. In one of the census records she list her maiden name as Smalls. However, when I was looking up the Michel family name, I kept coming across the last name of Rivers. I was so perplexed as to why that I asked one of the staff members at the South Carolina Historical Society and the gentleman informed me that it was because the two families Michel, and Rivers, had many business transactions between them. As I studied the transaction documents, I saw where the families had either bought and sold, or traded slaves. These were obviously the original white members of the two families. The white Michel's were probably Huguenots, French Europeans who transferred to the New World. The white Rivers turned out to be a prominent and wealthy Charleston family. Some of the Rivers had come to America, via the Caribbean Island of Barbados where they profited in the production of sugar cane using slave labor. The geographic origins of the Rivers family were in England. When they came to South Carolina they started a settlement on James Island called Riversville. The fact that the Michels and the Rivers traded in slaves with one another probably accounts for how my Great grandmother Willie Ann met my Great grandfather Samuel. However it happened, my Great Grandfather and Great Grandmother married and produced my grandmother Josephine along with several of her siblings. Just how many brothers and sisters my great grandmother Willie Ann had is sketchy. When my grandmother came of age and married my Grandfather David, they named their first born, (my aunt), Willie Ann after my great grandmother. My aunt Willie Ann passed away in 2011 at the age of 93. She was the eldest of my mom's sisters. With my aunt's passing, the mystery of how the name Willie Ann came into being has gone with her.

MY MATERNAL GREAT-GREAT GRANDFATHER MICHEL

MY GREAT-GREAT GRANDFATHER'S NAME was James Michel. (Samuels Father) In my research I was unable to come up with any pictures of him, just his name and address from the 1880 Census, which included the names of his wife and children. He had twin sons named James and Edward who were my great grandfather Samuels brothers. My great-great grandfather was listed in the census as having the occupation of Day-Laborer. It appears from the census records that he, his wife and children were living in the same house with his father in law and his family. Their names were Edward and Emma.

MY MATERNAL GREAT-GREAT GRANDMOTHER MICHEL/HOUSTON

MY MATERNAL GREAT-GREAT GRANDMOTHER'S name was Cecelia. (Samuels mother) My mother vaguely remembers her great grandmother as a distinguished woman who wore her hair in a long ponytail. And there was truth to her being distinguished. In my research I found records of her having a bank account with the Freedmens Bureau, a specialized bank set up to help former slaves establish a productive and meaningful life after the Civil War. The Freedmans Bank was established during the era of reconstruction. It seems that my great-great grandmother was also putting some money away for the benefit of her children. I saw her handwriting on one of the Freedman Bureau's documents and noted how her penmanship was impeccable. She was so far ahead of her time, especially for a woman in that day and age. So far I haven't found any records of her being a slave but she was definitely born during the era of slavery. Legend has it that she lived to be 103 years old.

My Maternal Great Great Great Grandfather Michel

I ONCE TOOK A trip to Salt Lake City Utah, and while I was there visited the Mormon Historical Family Library. Family is such an important part of the Mormon religion that they keep the most extensive family records found anywhere, and not just of their members but anyone. One young lady there helped me perform a search on one of their computers. I was able to find the listing of a name for my great great grandfather James's father. I was able to make a copy of it, however, I have lost that particular document. I have been racking my brain ever since trying to find it with no luck so far. So I know nothing about him, not even his name. I will try to visit Salt Lake City again to try and attain the record I once found mentioning him.

MY MATERNAL GREAT GREAT GREAT GRANDFATHER HOUSTON

MY GREAT GREAT GREAT grandfather Houston's (Cecelia's father) name was Isaac. The way I learned of him was not through the census but from the Freedmans Bureau records kept by my great great grandmother Cecelia. On the document it required the depositor (Cecelia) to list the name of her parents. She listed her father's name as Isaac Houston but next to his name she had written the word deceased. Other than his name, I have no information about my great great great grandfather Isaac. I tried to look up possible records about him, especially how he died but was unsuccessful.

My Maternal Great-Great-Great Grandmother Houston/Smith

My MATERNAL GREAT GREAT great grandmother's (Cecelia's mother) name was Emma. Emma and Isaac produced Cecelia and then from causes unknown to me Isaac passed away. However I found that Emma remarried. She married a man by the name of Edward Smith, making him Cecelia's Stepfather. I found records on Edward before I realized that he was not related to me. I discovered he was a former slave who'd been transferred to South Carolina from the island of Jamaica when he was only two years old. All I know about my great-great-great grandmother Emma is that she and her husband Edward shared a home with her daughter Cecelia and her husband James and their children in 1880.

Emma is listed in the 1880 census as being 45 years of age. That means that she was born approximately in 1835, which makes Emma the oldest known member of our family tree.

Now that I have recorded my definite ancestral lineage as far as I could, it is time to piece together the possible and most likely history of my family prior to the life of the oldest known member, Emma. In spite of having all of the odds against me due to the complexities of African American History, I have faced the challenges of those complexities head on in order to find the deepest roots of my family tree.

I will start with my father's side of the family, and the furthest back I was able to go was to the town of Glen Wilton where my father and possibly his mother was born.

GLEN WILTON HERITAGE

GLEN WILTON LIES BETWEEN the George Washington National Forest and the famous James River whose headwaters are about four miles northeast. The narrowest part of the James River approximately a mile south near the beginning of Woods Island, CSX railroad, James River division, runs parallel to the river. It has been said Glen Wilton is the only community in Virginia in which there are no public roads passing through the town. Mountain trails lead southwest to Roaring Run and north to Iron Gate.

Settlers came to the area in the 1700's. Native Americans formerly inhabited the area. With the building of the Buchanan and Clifton Forge Railroads in the 1880's, the train station was referenced as Wilton Depot. By 1890 the town was named Glen Wilton for the Glen sight it occupies and for Wilton Cook, the son of D. S. Cook, President of the Princess Furnace Company.

The Princess Iron Company formerly operated in Boyd County Kentucky had experienced many explosions during the period of its beginnings in 1876. It was dismantled in December of 1883 and moved to Wilton Station in Virginia and became a successful venture in the iron ore mining business. Company houses were built to accommodate the increasing population. The Princess Furnace was erected in 1884 and Iron ore mining was the chief industry in Glen Wilton until the furnace closed in 1923 having been forced out of business by the more economical Great Lakes Iron Ore operations.

In June 1941 the Triton Chemical Co. started operations of a TNT plant that was to employ a large number of people. They erected approximately seven buildings, numerous stands for tanks, spur tracks to the tanks, and used the Glen Wilton School as their office. This operation ceased in 1942 following an earth rocking blast of TNT at 3:39am on July 20. Two men along with a woman, and two children were killed and at least four others were hospitalized. The force of the explosion went downhill and away from the pack house. Had it affected the pack house, the loss would have been so devastating there would have been little left of the plant and even the community of Glen Wilton. As a result of the tragedy, the community was temporarily isolated as no one other than plant employees was permitted to come into Glen Wilton, not even the State Police. At the time of the explosion, the plant had been taken over by Hercules Powder Co. for the Army.

Mount Beulah Baptist, the Church my grandmother attended is located on land purchased by the Princess Furnace Co. The church is situated at the base of the mountains in Glen Wilton and was dedicated July 9 1909. There are only a few Black families left in Glen Wilton today compared to the many who lived there when the furnace was in operation. The cemetery located at the back of the church is where my grandmother is buried.

The first pastor was reverend A. A. Spencer of Buchanan. Other pastors since then have been the reverend W. Scott, O. W. Nolan, R.R. Terry, R. R. Banner, M. J. Robinson, and James Morgan who pastored from 1957 until 1985 and was from Covington. He served with his wife Annie Scott Morgan.

Past Deacons were James Lee Paul, Thomas Dan Richards, Haywood Brown, William Anderson, Edward Watson, John Leftwich, James Brown Sr. Asbury Anderson, Daniel Roach, and James Brown Jr. Thomas Dan Richards married my great grandmother Lucy Richards, but is not a blood relative.

In 1909 in the town of Glen Wilton in western Virginia, a murder allegedly committed by a black miner threatened to damage race relations between whites and all blacks in the community. Local blacks including several ministers met with concerned local whites. By posting signs warning that "all bad Negroes must quit town," the black community hoped to quell white concerns about black lawlessness. Local officials moved the alleged murderer to a safe jail, and tensions subsided. As one white later observed, "what's the use of having race trouble when the good Negroes want to be good?"

This is just about all of the information I have on my father's relatives, and their heritage in the town of Glen Wilton Virginia.

Next I will focus on my mother's side of the family and the experienced heritage of their lives.

CHARLESTON HERITAGE

WHEN AFRICAN AMERICANS ATTEMPT to look up slave records of their family members, most often they run into a brick wall of unreliable information. The reason being is that most of the slaves listed in the official records are listed by gender, age, shade of skin color, and whether or not they could read or write. Most often there are no names listed in the official records, and when the names are listed, they are first names only. This of course makes it difficult at best, and at worst impossible for anyone searching for slave ancestors. However there is one thing that African Americans can be sure of, and that is how our ancestors came to the land we now know as the United States of America. Some Africans came to these shores on slave ships directly from the African continent. However, some came via one or more stops along the slave trade route as my research showed was the most likely way some of my ancestors on my mother's side came to South Carolina.

I did dig up some slave records from the Michel's, and the River's families, but as I mentioned, only the gender, age and skin color was listed. In the few business transactions of slaves sold by the owners, only first names were shown. Therefore, I had no idea if I was looking at my ancestors or not. For most people that would be the end of the search but I was able to go further with the aid of modern technology. One day while on tour in Washington DC, I was visiting the National Geographic museum, and while I was in the gift shop I spotted a genealogy kit titled the Genographic Project. It was a project that National Geographic was conducting to help piece together human genealogy around the world and the main goal was to trace human geographic origins and migration patterns using the DNA of participants. Of course this grabbed my attention because even though I ran into a brick wall in terms of tracing my ancestors through historical records, this would be a means for me to trace my ancestral origins and migration pattern on the African Continent. So I purchased a kit, made the cheek swab and sent the kit in to be analyzed. National Geographic set it up so that participants could check online for the results. When the time came I checked the results and was astounded because they were exactly what I had expected.

If you read my first book, you would see that I had traveled to the African Continent well before I ever began to research my roots. It just so happens that the first country I visited in Africa was the country if Angola. I have traveled to the continent on three separate occasions visiting ten countries. On the second trip, one of the countries I visited was one that prior to going there I had not even heard of, the Island nation of Sao Tome. After visiting Sao Tome, I went to Ghana and saw two of several slave-holding fortresses used by slavers to hold the captives until they could be transported to the New World. One of the fortresses was Cape Coast, and the other was Elmina. It was while I was at Elmina that I discovered the historical records that showed that many of the slaves that were traded from Elmina, were brought there from Sao Tome.

When I researched the history of the slaves that were on the Island of Sao Tome, I found that they were brought to that Island from the country of Angola. The slaves went through a process called seasoning, which means that they were trained or broken from the lives they lived when they were free and taught how to be subservient slaves who answered to so called masters. In other words, the slavers first attempted to break the slaves spirit, then their backs. They were forced to do backbreaking work in places like the sugar cane fields of Sao Tome before being transferred to the New World.

If you look at the overall picture of this particular pattern, you can see how these Africans had first been taken from Angola, transferred to Sao Tome, and then transferred to Elmina before the final transfer to the New World. In my ancestors case it was Charleston South Carolina. So why do I believe that this was the particular route my ancestors traveled. Well, I have to say at this point that I believe every significant thing that happens to me in life happens for a reason. Yes this belief is spiritual in nature but you have to remember, one, I traveled to these places before I ever began researching my families history, that alone would be one heck of a coincidence. Two, when I did begin to do the research, the official historical records supported the theory or belief. For instance, in studying the documentary titled "Africans in America", as well as other historical documents, I discovered that Charleston South Carolina was not only the port were most Africans were landed in the America's, but during a certain time period, most of them were listed as Angolans. And third, the results of the DNA test that I took through National Geographic confirmed that my DNA matched those of Africans found in the areas of Angola and Sao Tome. Now I have historical, and scientific evidence to back what I had felt spiritually concerning my ancestral origins.

One interesting thing that came to mind was thinking about some of the historical events that took place during the time of my deceased ancestors. Specifically, where they were, and what they might have been doing when those historical events took place. I decided to start with the recent historical events that took place just before I was born then work my way back in time.

I'll start with the historic opera/musical "Porgy and Bess", based on a novel written by Dubose Heyward, with music by George Gershwin. The opera depicts African American life in Charleston South Carolina during the 1920s. My mother was born in 1919. Although the setting of Catfish Row is somewhat fictitious, the characters are based in part on the lives of real people. Dubose Heyward was a native of Charleston but Gershwin was unfamiliar with it so he went to James Island to get a feel for the life of African Americans in the Charleston area. It was while he was there that he gained the inspiration to write the music for "Porgy and Bess." He gained his musical inspirations for the opera from the Gullah speaking African Americans on the Island who'd preserved many of their African music traditions.

"Porgy and Bess" became very controversial especially among blacks due to elements of racism and by what most whites thought about African Americans during that time period. But not all black people looked upon the opera as negative. Some took it as a chance to use their talents, or to at least see themselves get some kind of exposure on the world's grand stages. Many famous black actors took the stage portraying various characters and singing songs throughout the shows production. People such as Billie Holiday, Ella Fitzgerald, Louis Armstrong, Miles Davis, John Coltrane, Sydney Poitier, Sammy Davis Jr., Dorothy Dandridge, Dianne Carroll, Pearl Bailey, Cab Calloway, and Maya Angelou.

It would be one thing for me to be curious about what my ancestors were doing around the time that the original opera was being produced, but the fact that they were in this location during that particular time is intriguing to say the least. Through research I know that my ancestors were in Charleston but also that my great grandmother Willie Ann who most likely descended from slaves owned by the Rivers family. The Rivers family owned plantations on James Island. As I mentioned earlier, Porgy and Bess was based in part on the lives of real people, one of them being the main character Porgy, a black disabled beggar who falls in love with Bess the other main Character. Although there is some controversy surrounding whether or not Bess was a real person, it is a fact that Porgy was based on a real man who's true name was Samuel (Sammy) Smalls. What makes this so significant to me is that at one time I thought my great grandmother Willie Ann's maiden name was Rivers, but through research I came across a certificate of live birth of one of Willie Ann's children where she had to list her maiden name, and she'd listed that name as Smalls. So of course my question is, was Samuel Smalls the man whose life was used to develop the character Porgy one of my relatives? Maybe, and maybe not. I do know through interviewing my aunt that my grandfather David Thomas knew the owner of the New York City night club Smalls Paradise, and that my aunt said that he was also from Charleston South Carolina. If you watch the movie Malcom X there is a scene where Malcom enters Smalls Paradise. So even though I cannot be certain, it is a possibility that through my ancestors, I could be connected to that part of history.

The next area of history I would like to explore as it relates to my ancestry is the period during reconstruction and slavery. Following the Civil War, the U.S. government set up the Freedmans Bureau, an organization dedicated to helping former slaves make the transition from chattel slavery to being a free people. The Bureau was initiated by then President Abraham Lincoln and was in existence from 1865-1872. The Freedmans Bureau assisted the former slaves by aiding them with food, housing, education, employment, and healthcare. Whenever it was possible, the bureau also helped ex slaves reunite with family members who had been sold during slavery. By enlisting the aid of the Freedmans Bureau, some slaves were putting their lives in danger because many southern whites hated the Bureau because they claimed it was helping blacks organize against their former masters. There were indeed several clashes between some southern whites and black members of the Freedmans Bureau.

The significance of the Freedmans Bureau in terms of my family's lineage is the fact that my great great grandmother Cecelia was a documented member of the Freedmans Bureau Bank. This means that it is highly likely that she was a former slave trying to take advantage of the new right to make the transition to freedom. Although the bank was established in

1865, I could only find records of my great great grandmothers membership during the years of 1871 and 1872 the final years of the established bureau. The Freedmans Savings Bank had several presidents, but its last and most famous was the former slave, orator, and abolitionist Frederick Douglas. At the height of the banks success, it had assets of more than $3.7 million, The bank is very important in the study of African American History because with its list of 480,000 names, it is the largest single repository of lineage linked African American records. Of the 480,000 names listed, only 61,131 names are recorded as depositors. And my great great grandmother Cecelia Michel is one of them.

Cecillia's Signature

DOCUMENTS

RETURN OF A BIRTH. 810

To the Board of Health, City of Charleston, S.C.

MASTICK STREET.

1. Full Name of Child (if any) — William Henry Michel
2. Sex — Mail   No. of Child of Mother — 5
3. Race or Color, (if not of the white races) — Color'd
4. Date — Sept 3 1900
5. Place of Birth — 42 Aston St
6. Full Name of Mother — Willie Ann Michel
   (Maiden Name) — Smalls
7. Mother's Birthplace — Charleston S.C.
8. Mother's Residence — 42 Aston St
9. Full Name of Father — Samuel Michel
10. Father's Occupation — Cooper
11. Father's Birthplace — Charleston, S.C.
Name of Medical Attendant —
Name of Person who makes this Return — Harden Oddings
Date of this Return — Sept 4

Willie Ann Maiden name (Smalls)

	Name			Relation			Occupation
	Graham Saving	B M 34	Brother-in-law				Daylaborer
69	Tally Mary	Mu F 34			/		Keeping House
	Mitchell John	Mu M 8	Nephew	/			
20	Smith Emma	B F 55			/		Keeping House
	Smith Edward	Mu M 53	Husband		/		Cooper
	Michel James	B M 36	Son-in-law		/		Daylaborer
	Michel Cecilia	B F 80	Daughter		/		At home
	Smith Harriett	Mu F 15	Niece	/			At home
	Aveilhie Emma	Mu F 10	Granddaughter	/			At home
	Aveilhie Ella	Mu F 5	Granddaughter	/			
	Aveilhie Arthur	Mu M 11	Grandson	/			At home
	Aveilhie Willie	Mu M 7	Grandson	/			At home
	Michel James	B M 11	Grandson	/			At home
	Michel Edward	B M 11	Grandson	/			At home
	Michel Samuel	B M 8	Grandson	/			
	Miller Charles	Mu M 53			/		Daylaborer
	Miller Sarah	B F 48	Wife		/		Washerwoman
	Miller Samuel	Mu M 21	Son	/			Daylaborer
	Miller Robert	M M 11	Son	/			At home

1880 Census

Newspaper Advertisment

CONNECTICUT MUTUAL LIFE INSURANCE C

THE FINEST HOME-DRESSED RE-
FRIGERATOR MEATS
FOR SALE BY
—TELEPHONE 577.—

NELSON & MUNZENMAIER,
629 KING STREET.

MIC   607   MID

Michel John P, clk H J O'Neill, r 107 Church
Michel Lawrence A, student, r 107 Church
Michel Marie Miss, private school, r 68 Cannon
Michel Samuel *c* (Ann), cooper, r 42 Ashton
Michel William F, clk So Ry, r 4 Doughty
Mickens Amos *c* (Caroline), lab, r 176 Smith
Mickey Charles A *c*, barber 3 Drake, r 42 Alexander
MICKEY EDWARD H (Estate), Christopher Hayne
mngr, undertaker and embalmer 259 Meeting   See advt
Mickey Hannah *c*, r 37 Rose la
Mickle Edward *c* (Augustus), wks O M Terry, r 5 Hughes ct

TABLE 45

SLAVES IMPORTED INTO THE NORTH AMERICAN MAINLAND, BY ORIGIN

Coastal region of origin	Per cent of slaves of identifiable origin imported by			
	(1) Virginia, 1710–69	(2) South Carolina, 1733–1807	(3) British slave trade, 1690–1807	(4) Speculative estimate, all imported into North America (%)
Senegambia	14.9	19.5	5.5	13.3
Sierra Leone	5.3	6.8	4.3	5.5
Windward Coast	6.3	16.3	11.6	11.4
Gold Coast	16.0	13.3	18.4	15.9
Bight of Benin	—	1.6	11.3	4.3
Bight of Biafra	37.7	2.1	30.1	23.3
Angola	15.7	39.6	18.2	24.5
Mozambique-Madagascar	4.1	0.7	*	1.6
Unknown	—	—	0.6	0.2
Total	100.0	100.0	100.0	100.0

* Included in Angola figure.
Sources: Table 43, col. 13; Donnan, *Documents*, 4, *passim*. See text, p. 156.

Slave Import Statistics into South Carolina from Angola

WHERE IT BEGAN

Slave Fortress Ghana, West Africa

Slave holding cell Ghana West Africa

FAMILY PHOTOS

Mom as a baby

My mom & Dad in New York

My mom holding me

Next of course is the era of the Civil War. When you look up the definition for the word civil in the dictionary, you will find several terms. For instance I found: "of or relating to citizens, and of or relating to the state or its citizenry, adequate in courtesy and politeness: Mannerly, of or relating to, or based on civil law, of, relating to, or involving the general public, their activities, needs, or ways, or civic affairs as distinguished from special affairs such as religious, or military." I find it strange that that particular war was called "The Civil War." There really was nothing civil about it, especially when you consider the reason for fighting it. I know historians and others say that it was fought because of economics, States rights, etc. But the truth of the matter is the so-called civil war was fought over the issue of slavery. Whether or not one human being has the right to put another human being into bondage, specifically to be used as a means of income without any inherent God given rights, let alone compensation, was the cause of the war. Those who believe in the confederate way of life will look you in the eye and state that they believe God himself gave them the right to own another human being, based on that person's culture and race. Yet not one of them would want to suffer the same fate. In other words, it's ok for others, but don't treat them that way. Somehow the words "Do Unto Others As You Would Have Them Do Unto You" have no real meaning to them. If you look at the numerical statistic of the Civil War, you will find that over 600,000 people lost their lives fighting it. That translates to over one million gallons of human blood spilled for that cause. And that is not counting the blood spilled by those who were wounded.

I have often wondered where my ancestors where and what they were doing during the war that was fought in part for them. Through research I have come across clues to where some of them, namely my great grandmother Willie Ann's parents and grandparents were at the time. Through more research I have found some information on the white Rivers family that I believe were the former owners of my great grandmother Willie Ann's relatives, and my ancestors. Records show that the first Rivers to inhabit this part of Low Country South Carolina lived on a plantation on James Island, a sea island just off of Charleston. The man's name was William Rivers and he settled there around 1694. William Rivers built a home near where the Wappoo Creek meets the Ashely River. Even though I believe that the Rivers owned my great grandmother Willie Ann's family, the problem is that there were several Rivers family members that settled in the area after the original member William. In fact after settling on James Island, William sent word to several family members to come to South Carolina from Bermuda. I researched many of them and came up with some of their names. So far I found William, the first Rivers to inhabit the area, and it is said the first Rivers family member to come to America. William Rivers had no male descendents, but his many brothers and cousins whom he sent for did. Then there was another William Rivers (1775-1837), in fact I found several William Rivers. The following names are some but not necessarily in any order of arrival or kinship. One relative was Constant Horace Rivers the son of the aforementioned William, born in 1829 and died in 1910. In 1851he planned and developed the village of Riversville. He married Mary Elizabeth Minott. From the data I gathered it appears they had nine children. Their names were: William Constant Rivers born in 1850, Susan Ann Rivers born November 16, 1851, and died 6 months later on May 27, 1852, William Edings Rivers born in 1853 who lived only to the age of one year and six months, John Minot Rivers born April 13, 1855 and died May 9, 1929, Horace Rivers born in 1857, Fraser M. Rivers born in 1860, William Constant Rivers born April 15, 1865 and died July 27, 1927, Moultrie Rutledge Rivers born May 16, 1868 and died February 23, 1940, and finally Arthur Lee Rivers born September 10, 1870 an died May 13, 1845. All of the children appear to have been born on James Island. Constant Horace Rivers had 16 slaves.

Then there was a William Horace Rivers, (Constant's brother) born around 1817 and died on October 23, 1861 at the age of 44. He married Sarah Bailey Jenkins born in 1816 and died on July 3, 1895 at the age of 79. William and Sarah had eight children, their names are as follows: William born in 1840 in Charleston, Martha Jenkins Rivers born on August 28th 1841 in Charleston and died 81 days later, Charles H. Rivers, born October 27, 1843 in Charleston and died May 5, 1912, Susan A. Rivers born in 1848 in Charleston, Sarah R. Rivers in 1843 on James Island and died August 10, 1907, Ella T. born in 1852 on James Island, John D. Rivers born in 1852 on James Island, and Emile E. born in 1854 on James Island. William Horace Rivers had 40 slaves in which 3 were listed as admitted to communion in church. Their names were Ginny, Charlotte, and Hetty.

For now I am going stop here because although there are others, I believe I have found a Rivers, or perhaps even the Rivers that May have a direct connection to my ancestors during the time of the Civil War and even further back to Slavery and the possible beginning of a branch of my people's entry into the America's.

The name I have the most interest in, at least for now is William Horace Rivers. Why this particular Rivers? Well so far he is the only one who I have found on record to have business dealings with the Michels, the other part of my family tree. Through painstaking research at the South Carolina Historical Society, I found documents spelling out business transaction between the two families, namely between the estates of William Horace Rivers and an Angeline Michel. In the case of Angeline Michel, I found a transaction that said only "cash paid you at this date $50 September 26, 1854, and in parenthesis (by Mrs. Rivers) R: No 30". Then another by her Estate in 1853 that read "amount in interest on William Horace Rivers bond carried to (illegible) $169.44." On the account of William Horace Rivers, I found a document that read "May 15, 1863 Trust Est.: Michel wife bond principle & interest $5789.05." Even by today's standards $5789.05 is a substantial amount of money. For the mid 1800's it was definitely a significant amount, which leads me to believe that it was more than likely used for slave trading. The reason I came to this conclusion is because of historical data I found concerning the planters of Riversville on James Island and the value of their property, which included slaves. For instance, in the year 1860, the typical Riversville cotton planter had an average capital investment of $61,710 in his plantation. Of that, 36.6% ($22,605) was invested in land, and 63.4% ($39,115) was invested in slaves. An acre of agricultural land on James Island was valued at approximately $37.24, whereas the average slave had a value of $620.87. As an ancestor of African slaves brought to this continent, I cannot stress enough the significance of these findings. William Horace Rivers a possible owner of a branch of my slave ancestors had 300 acres of land valued at $10,000, yet his 40 slaves commanded a value of $26,000. William B. Seabrook one of if not the largest landowner on James Island had 1,230 acres valued at $50,000, and 123 slaves valued at over $100,000. Eight members of the planters associated with Riversville owned a total of 4,861 acres of land valued at $181,000, and 503 slaves whose value commanded $347,000, almost twice the value of the land.

If African American slaves and freeman had never fought in any war from the Revolutionary to the Civil, (and they did) their significant value and overwhelming contribution to the growth, prosperity, and great standing of the United States would still be unquestionable.

It is more than likely that William Horace Rivers was the owner of a branch of my ancestors, and therefore they would have been slaves on one of the Rivers plantations on James Island. That means that during the Civil War they were either on James Island or in Charleston. So looking at the Civil War events that took place around Charleston and in particular James Island I can get an image of what they may have witnessed. The historical records show that on December 20, 1860 South Carolina voted to secede from the Union. In a weeks time Union soldiers stationed at Fort Moultrie on Sullivan's Island moved by boat to Fort Sumter where they thought they would have a better chance of protecting themselves when the inevitable war started. The confederacy immediately took over the abandoned Fort Moultrie, Castle Pinckney, and Fort Johnson on James Island, not far from the Rivers plantation. The Confederate military constructed cannon batteries on the Islands surrounding Fort Sumter. One of those batteries was on Morris Island, and another at Fort Johnson on James Island where historians say the actual first shot of the Civil War occurred.

On April 10, 1861 Confederate President Jefferson Davis sent word to General Beauregard to demand the surrender of Fort Sumter. The demands were issued on the 11th however, they were refused by the Union Army leader stationed at the fort. On a rainy morning at around 2:10am on the 12th the confederates fired the first shot of the Civil War from Fort Johnson on James Island.

The records show that most of the common people left the area of the fighting and sought shelter in Charleston. However, when they left and whether or not the evacuations included the slaves is sketchy at best. So if the slaves remained, or where still there during the opening shots of the war, this means that a branch of my ancestors could very well have witnessed the beginning of the Civil War.

I also found out that two of the most recognized battles in which James Island played a vital part was the "Battle of Secessionville", and the "Battle for Fort Wagner" made famous by the movie "Glory". The "Battle of Secessionville" lasted approximately one month and was fought across the Rivers plantation. The battle started on May 19, 1862 and when it ended there were only two buildings left standing. The reason the battle was so fierce is because between the Union and the Confederacy, whichever side won this particular battle could very well determine the length, if not the outcome of the war. The reason being is that Charleston was known as the backdoor to the confederacy, and therefore if overtaken by the Union, the supplies for the confederate Army would be severely disrupted. Also, the battle of Fort Wagner was significant to African American History in that one group of soldiers who fought in that particular battle were an all volunteer unit made up of black soldiers from the 54th Massachusetts Regiment. The regiment was under the command of

Colonel Robert Gould Shaw. Fort Wagner was named after a confederate colonel, Thomas Wagner who had gained notoriety for repelling an attack by union troops at Secessionville, a battle that my ancestors may have witnessed because it was fought across one of the Rivers plantations. In fact, a temporary confederate command post was set up on the Rivers plantation during the battle. Fort Wagner was located on Morris Island and was needed by the Union because of its strategic location. The Union amassed several thousands of soldiers for the assault on Fort Wagner and bombarded the Fort heavily beforehand. During the preparation for the assault, several skirmishes between the Union and the rebels took place on nearby James Island with the 54th Massachusetts being involved. It was the first time the unit had engaged in combat and it is said they fought gallantly. Over 30 were killed and 14 captured. The first attack by Union troops on Fort Wagner was repelled and the Union had to regroup and wait for nightfall to try another assault. To show what they were up against, the confederates had batteries located at strategic positions covering Fort Wagner. So when the Union troops assaulted they not only had to go against the barrage of bullets coming from the fort itself, but they also had to endure mortar fire coming from the surrounding confederate batteries on James Island. At around 8:00pm the Union troops came out of their earthworks and began the assault. They were led by the all volunteer all black 54th Massachusetts under their leader Colonel Shaw. Nightfall meant high tide, and they had to trudge through knee-deep water on their way to the fortification. Many were mowed down in the hale of gun and mortar fire. But some made it through the parapets, over the wall and into the fort where fierce hand-to-hand combat took place. So many Union soldiers were killed that the bodies were piled on top of one another at the parapets. In the end, neither the 54th Massachusetts nor any other Union unit was able to take the fort. Before the battle, the 54th marched through the streets of Charleston as proud black men, some of the first to wear the uniform of the Union, which represented their right to live free or die fighting for that freedom. Now I, a descendent of slaves who were there, wonder if my ancestors witnessed these men marching and or fighting for a future that would see them as well as myself, living free.

South Carolina, and James Island in particular were areas of extreme wealth prior to the Civil War. One observer noted that James Island plantations looked like seas of white cotton. However, during the late 1800's after the war, the James Island planters along with planters of the other sea-islands were experiencing a state of economic collapse. The war had taken its toll on those who wrung their bread from the sweat of the slave's foreheads. Left with only the destruction of their buildings and abandoned muddy fields, the planters attempted to return their lands to the days of prosperity prior to the Civil war. The attempts were thwarted first by an epidemic of small pox and yellow fever. After the epidemic subsided, a man by the name of Elias Rivers produced a high yield cotton seed that brought the Island back to prosperity for a time until a setback by an infestation of the boll weevil. The James Island planters never again experienced the kind of prosperity they had enjoyed prior to the Civil War.

As I mentioned earlier, in my research of my family history, I have come across documents that describe the sale of goods and property, including slaves by members of the Rivers family. Some of the transactions were prior to the Civil War, yet others were clearly dated after it had ended. It appears that the Rivers Klan along with the other sea island planters were selling off land and property in order to survive the devastation mostly caused by the war. The documents show business transactions between a Mrs. Angeline Michel and a Mr. John E. Rivers, as well as the estate of William Horace Rivers and one of the Michel wives, whom is not known because the papers read only "trust estate of Michel wife bond & principle $5789.05." The date of that particular document shows that the transaction took place on May 15, 1863. Although this is before the war ended, by 1863 the war was clearly taking its toll on southern planters because even if they were still producing crops, they found it hard to sell because of the Union blockades. Much of the cotton the planters produced prior to the war was sold to Great Britain. However, the British abolished the slave trade prior to the abolition of slavery in the United States. Therefore the British were no longer buying cotton from the south and that was clearly hurting the southern planters financially. One of the things about the documents that caught my attention was that on a couple of them the dates show that the Rivers and the Michel's had been doing business with each other at least as far back as 1853. That includes the selling and buying of slaves. So my question of course is one, where the Rivers the first purchasers of that particular branch of my ancestors after arriving from Africa? And two, did the Rivers sell one or several of that branch of my ancestors to the Michel's, or did my great grandmother Willie Ann simply come into contact with my great grandfather Samuel through the association of the two families. Or, did my great grandparents just happen to meet by chance. Well, it is my strong feeling that they met somehow through the association of the two families. (The Rivers and the Michels)

This brings me to the period of time prior to the Civil War. When the sea Islands, James Island in particular were being developed for agricultural purposes, the land obviously had to be cleared. When the planters first purchased their respective properties they found land that was infested with venomous snakes, crocodiles as big as 16 feet long, and disease ridden insects. Of course the people who had to do the actual clearing of the land were the slaves. Although the snakes and crocodiles were a factor, the real obstacles were the insects because of disease. During several periods of time there were outbreaks of yellow fever and malaria on the Islands. This brings me to a point of research that explains how the slaves were able to deal with the harshness of these diseases along with all the other harsh realities of being a slave. When I researched the disease of malaria, I found that it was and still is very prevalent in certain countries around the world but especially in sub Saharan Africa. In fact the area that my ancestors come from Angola, is currently second in the entire world when it comes to fatalities from the disease of malaria. What I found was that the Africans who came from this area and other areas where malaria was and is prevalent, had a natural genetic resistance to malaria. That genetic resistance was built into the cell structure of the slaves. However since the transfer of Africans from their native land to the America's, that natural cell structured resistance has somehow turned from a protection to a deadly disease we call sickle cell. I have had at least two family members that I know of who died from complications of sickle cell.

I now somewhat understand what my ancestors endured as slaves toiling from day to day for no pay and no reward, no fruit from their hard labor and a big question mark in terms of what life in the future would bring. But of even more interest to me is trying to wrap my mind around what my ancestors went through from the moment they were captured in their homeland, through being marched to the dark and dank holding pens, to being hauled aboard the ship that would take them across the Atlantic Ocean. Then to be landed in a place that would change their entire being from men and women, to nothing more than property with no rights that any white man or woman would have to respect. So many questions! What were their real names? What language did they speak? How did they summon the strength to endure all of the pain and suffering of laying in the dark putrid smelling, suffocating bowels of a constantly rocking ship for 60 to 90 days? What were they doing just before being captured? It could have been by white men with guns or by Africans who it is known took their enemies as captives and sold them into slavery. This is something that we as African Americans don't like to face when dealing with the history of slavery, but it is a fact and needs to be dealt with. We have to deal with it because it tells us that sometimes we can be our own worst enemy. And, more importantly, if we don't learn from the past, the same mistakes can and will be repeated in the present and future. Don't get me wrong! I am in no way letting the whites that perpetuated the system of slavery off the hook. After all, two wrongs don't make it right. There is enough blame to go around. I will say this; we're all dirty, but it sure would be nice to get clean.

Finally I wonder if they would be proud of me, and if they have been able to live some of their dreams through me? One of the most important things I can say I learned from them is in knowing that they endured all of the toil, agony, and suffering through slavery and still survived so that I could exist. So what was it that they actually endured besides some of the things that I've already mentioned? Well in detail, I researched some of the statistics on the shear brutality of slavery and they are as follows: When the slave trade peaked between 1751 and 1800, about ten thousand slaves died annually during the Atlantic crossing to the Americas. Many slaves were captured inland, sometimes hundreds of miles from the coast. They were marched to the coast shackled by chains many times in groups of about fifty. Many died on the long hot miserable march to the coast. Their capture was accomplished by raiding parties whom would sneak into a village and kidnap as many of its people as possible, and sometimes the whole village would be subdued. I can only imagine the horror, and frightening shock of being raided, kidnapped and marched to an unknown destination for an unknown reason. Once the slaves reached the coast, they were placed in barracoons, (holding pens) or fortresses where they were forced to wait sometime as long as a year, and fed little food and water until the arrival of the slave ship. They were placed in the holding pens where the men and women were separated. At some point in time while they were waiting, some of the kidnappers would brand the men, woman and children with a hot branding iron This was the first act of laying claim to them as now being slaves, transferred from being humans with rights, to someone's property, with no rights whatsoever. I dare anyone to try and imagine the pain, mental as well as physical, of being branded on the bare skin with a hot iron. Then their heads were shaved, sometimes men and women. Their clothes were stripped off and some lay totally naked while waiting to be taken onto the ship. The slaves were then examined as if they were animals being prepared for sale. The examiners would inspect their teeth, skin, muscle structure, and even the private parts of men, women, and children, as they stood naked in front of total strangers. Twice as many men as women were taken. The records show an estimated 67% men, and 32% women. The rest were children. The women who were kept in separate holding pens were often sexually abused by their captures, especially the managing overseers of the fortress or holding pen. Then the Africans were loaded onto the ships that were designed to hold 200 souls. However, for the sake of increased profits the slavers would load these ships with anywhere from 300 to 600 slaves. These humans were packed sometimes laying down, and sometimes in sitting positions. Whatever the position, they were packed tightly next to one another. It was bad enough that the slaves were packed together tightly, but when you consider that they were below the ships decks where there was no light, and very little breathable air, it becomes unimaginable. Cleanliness of the ship, and the hygiene of its human cargo depended upon the ships captain, and or the demands of the owners. It came to a point where the owners and ships captains began to realize the importance of caring for the African slaves. In other words, the more care that was given to the Africans, the better the chances were that they would survive the long voyage. This obviously resulted in increased profits for all involved. However, this was not always the case, especially in the beginning. The start of the African Transatlantic Slave Trade was basically a free for all with very little thought for the welfare of the Africans as it related to the end results of profits. On many occasions in the beginning, not enough food was stored for the slaves during the Middle Passage of the voyage. This was most often because more slaves were packed onto the ship then it was designed to hold. When the captains realized that there would not be enough food, they often resorted to gathering some of the Africans who were sick or just chosen at random and while still chained together have the crew throw them overboard. Once in the water, they would either drown or be eaten by sharks. Sometimes the other slaves were allowed to watch this brutal act as a way of warning them against any thoughts of rebellion. If the slaves had any doubts about the inhumane brutal nature of their captors, this act would usually eliminate those doubts. The other thing the slaves had to contend with is disease. The filthy conditions of the slave vessels were an incubator for killer diseases. As I mentioned, the slaves were stacked over one another by deck planks. When the ship was under way, many of the slaves became sea sick. This would obviously cause them to vomit. The slaves would naturally have to expend their waste and because they were only brought up on the main deck occasionally, had to go upon themselves. It does not take a great imagination to know that the vomit, feces, and urine would fall onto the slaves below. They were chained there with no way of avoiding this insane condition. Obviously this caused an unnatural condition of horrid filth that perpetuated disease. The food the slaves were fed usually consisted of beans, rice, cassava, and every now and then some salted pork. All of this food was kept in dark, hot, humid storage compartments. A lot of this food, especially what was used for the slaves would go bad, and this too contributed to the toll taken from disease on the slaves as well as the crew.

Some of the African women were pregnant during the voyage to the new world. Sometimes they were pregnant prior to being captured, but other times they became pregnant as a result of sexual abuse by their captures before they boarded the ship, or by the crew after they were onboard. I have given you part of a visual image of what took place during the African Atlantic Slave Trade, and allowed you to imagine the horrid smells. But, I have not talked about the assault that would have taken place upon a slave's ears, namely the screams, of the woman, the cries of the children, and moans of the men. In no way could a contemporary human's imagination come close to the psychological affect of such an experience. In researching the Atlas of the Transatlantic Slave trade, I saw that the graph showing the number of slaves departing from Africa is greater than the number of arrivals at any given port. This is due to the deaths of some of the Africans while on the voyage. As far as I can tell, there were approximately 800,000 African slaves who lost their lives due to the cruelty they endured during the Atlantic crossing. Many historians believe that to be a low figure, and that there were many more deaths due to the crossing than what I just described. The following is from some documented records I researched from the volume of The "Transatlantic Slave Trade."

Date died	Days Sick	Description of person	Cause of death
14 Nov 179	12	Boy	Fever
26 Nov 1791	37	Woman	Chest complaint
8 Apr 1792	60	Girl	Dysentery
7 Jul 1792	2	Man	Fever
12 Aug 1792	13	Woman	Scurvy
20 Jun 1719	?	Man	Epilepsy
9 Jun 1719	?	Boy	Convulsions
29 Jun 1719	?	Woman	Violent blow to the head
1 Aug 1792	?	Man	Drowned
26 Nov 1791	22	Woman	Hysteria
9 May 1792	?	Woman	Hemorrhage of the Uterus

This brutality is what the slaves including my ancestors had to endure, and all of it was suffered even before they were landed into the world of plantations.

When they arrived in places like Charleston, they were removed from the ship and placed into another holding pen. The slave traders would prepare them for sale by feeding and fattening them up a bit. They would also give crude medical attention to wounds they received during the harsh ocean passage, and afterward oil their skin before they were presented to potential slave buyers. On the day of the slave auction the slaves who had not died from the voyage would be taken and placed onto auction blocks and sold like cattle. But before being purchased, they were once again stripped naked and inspected for their ability to handle the harsh and brutal labor they would soon have to face. After inspection, they were sold to the highest bidder. When the new slave owner took the slave or slaves into his possession, they were often branded again for proof of whom it was they now belonged. After enduring the pain of another hot iron branding, the slaves were tied to a wagon and sometimes made to walk the long distance to the plantation that would be their new home.

On the plantation, the slaves would be trained in their new task of working from sunup to sundown. But not before being persuaded that they now had a new name, and that name was whatever the master said it was. If they should have a hard time pronouncing the new name because of the language barrier, they were given extra encouragement by way of a whip to get it right. They learned that they were not allowed to have intimate relations with the opposite sex without the master's permission. They could not marry without the master's permission. If allowed to be married, they were in constant fear of being separated because at any given time the so-called master could sell one of them and they may never see one another again. The master had so much power that he or she could even sell the slaves children away from them. If the slave put up the least bit of protest, he or she could be beaten severely. When they worked in the field producing whatever crop brought profit to the master, they did not receive sick days or even reasonable breaks. They learned to eat while they worked. They learned to pronounce their new names, and they learned to keep themselves warm in a winter season they had not previously known. Then dealt with the sweltering humid heat of a plantation summer. They adapted a way of not letting themselves get too close emotionally so that it wouldn't hurt so bad if they were sold away from one another. Somehow, some way, the slaves, my ancestors, held on and endured everything that was forced upon them.

So whom do I blame for this unspeakable tragedy? In some ways I blame no one, and in many ways I blame everyone. For me, this is not just a lesson for those who created the brutal system of the Atlantic slave trade. Nor is it just a lesson for the Africans who helped make it possible. No, it is far bigger than that. This to me is a lesson for the world about the potential for man's inhumanity to his fellow man. We all have a responsibility to fight against the evils of inhumane treatment against any human being no matter who is promoting it, or who the victims of it may be.

I cannot fathom how my ancestors endured so much. But I am sworn for the rest of my life to show gratitude because they did.

Now, whenever I am going through a hard time, whether it is physical or mental, as always I look to my creator, but also the strength of my ancestors. I realize that nothing I am going through can possibly come close to what they had to endure. The slave traders would not, and could not take slaves from among the weakest of Africans. They knew that physically and mentally, only the strongest could survive that system. What that means to me is that spiritually, mentally, and physically, I come from the strongest of the strong. And I will not dishonor their sacrifices by being weak. So no matter what, I press on through life.

Like in my first book's dedication, I end this perhaps my last book with hopes of inspiration for my offspring who may question whether or not our lives are based on a matter of fate? I leave you with the inspirational, yet challenging words of Barrack Obama, the first African American President of the United States: "Our destiny is not determined for us, but by us."

So it was, so it is, and so it will be, for all of our Generations.

GENERATIONS is a book about the author's search for his ancestors. The book traces the author's genealogy back through slavery. As the author states; we cannot possibly know ourselves, let alone know where we are going until we are willing to first take the time to learn from where, and from whom we have come.

Like many, the author grew up attending public schools and hating history. However, as he matured, a paradigm shift in his thoughts concerning history occurred. Through this book, the author inspires and encourages others to understand the importance of the past, in particular, their own. But more importantly is the author's desire to get readers to understand society's critical need to learn from our ancestors through knowledge of what they got wrong, and to gain strength and hope from the things they did right.

ISBN 978-1-4817-1716-8

51395

9 781481 717168